Sophie

TRIES *Again*

WRITTEN BY PAM BURGESS
ILLUSTRATED BY AANU DAVID

Sophie Tries Again
Book 3 of the Sophie Series
Copyright 2023 by Pam Burgess | pamburgess.com
Illustrated by Aanu David
Published by Argyle Fox Publishing | argylefoxpublishing.com
ISBN 978-1-953259-44-8 (Paperback)
ISBN 978-1-953259-43-1 (Hardcover)

The jump rope rested in Sophie's hands. She was ready to try again.

"Ok, here we go."

Sophie lifted her right foot and balanced on her left leg. She swung the rope high overhead. As the rope came down, Sophie jumped, but the rope caught around her foot.

"I can't believe it," she cried in a tangle of jump rope. "I tried and tried, and I just can't do it!"

Sophie stomped her bunny
feet on the ground and threw
the rope across the yard.

Sophie's mom watched from the window.
"There she goes again," she said as the jump rope sailed across the lawn.

"What are you looking at?" Sophie's dad asked.

Sophie's mom pointed out the window. "She threw the jump rope again. She gets so frustrated when she tries something and it doesn't turn out the way she wants it to."

"Well, I know that feeling," Sophie's dad said. "I tried a jump with my skateboard when I was young, and I fell more times than I could count!"

He looked out the window, but he didn't see Sophie. He saw himself as a young rabbit.

"I just couldn't get the jump right," he said. "Actually, I still feel that way sometimes, when I'm trying to do something hard."

Sophie sat on the ground,
arms crossed and face angry.
"Why don't you talk to her?"
Sophie's Mom suggested.

Sophie scowled as her dad approached.
"I can't do it!" she announced. "I'm just not
good enough. I try and try to do a loop de
loop like Annie, but I just get tangled up in the
rope. I give up!"

Sophie's Dad settled down
beside her.
"I know how you feel," he
said. "It's hard to try and try
and fail."

Sophie looked at her Dad in surprise. "What do you mean?" she asked. "You don't fail. You're a grown-up, and stuff's easy for you. I'm just a kid."

"Well," he said with a laugh, "I've not always been a grown-up. When I was your age I wanted to do the phoenix flutter with my skateboard, like my friend Lochlan could." Sophie's Dad stood up. "You have to lean back on one foot—like this—and use your other foot to control the front of your skateboard—like this."

He pointed his toe forward and put his arms in front of him. Then he dropped his arms to his sides and sighed.

"I tried and tried and tried," he said, "but I just couldn't seem to do it. I would fall down, scrape my knees, and get so angry,"

"Just like me?" Sophie said.

"Angry enough that I would kick my skateboard as hard as I could."

"What?" Sophie said. "You did lots of skateboard jumps when you were a kid. You told Mom and me about them!"

"Oh, yes, I did," Sophie's Dad replied, "but it took a lot of practice before I could do any jumps at all! To be honest, I wanted to give up long before I could do the phoenix flutter."

"So why didn't you?" Sophie asked. "Why didn't you give up?"

"Well, one day I was with Lochlan at the skateboard park. He was doing all kinds of tricks. I was sitting on the bench feeling particularly frustrated.

Mr. Owliver flew over and landed on the bench next to me." Sophie's dad's eyes sparkled at the memory. "He asked what was wrong, and I told him. After a moment, Mr. Owliver asked, 'What would you dooo differently, if you thought you could dooo it?' And then, as he always does, he flew away."

Sophie laughed. Mr. Owliver has done the same thing for a long time. "So what did you do?" Sophie asked.

Sophie's Dad leaned toward Sophie. "I thought about what Mr. Owliver said—for a long time. I thought I could do the flutter, so I decided to keep trying until I did it." He stood up to demonstrate. "I tried different ways to stand and different ways to move my arms. I tried and tried until I figured it out, because I knew I could do it."

Sophie giggled as her dad dropped to the grass.
"So you just did it?"

"Not as easy as that. I had to practice and try
some different things, and fall some more. But," he
said, "I kept thinking about what Mr. Owliver said,
and I knew I could do it if I just kept trying."

The sun broke through the trees.
Sophie tilted her head back to warm her
face. Sophie's Dad scratched her ear.

"Finally," he said, "I did the phoenix flutter and then many other jumps after that, but they all took a lot of practice. And by the way, grown-ups don't always get it right the first time."

Sophie's dad pulled two apples from his pocket. He handed one to Sophie.

"Hungry?"

Sophie took the bright green apple and munched on the delicious snack with her father.

Later that day, the sun began hiding behind the hillside. Sophie had just finished dinner. She grabbed the firm handles of her bright pink jump rope and walked outside.

She was on one foot, swinging the rope.
"Ahhhhh!"
Her legs tangled in the rope.

"Okay," she said to the forest, "this isn't working. So, what did Dad say? If I know I can do it, I should keep trying different things until I get it right."

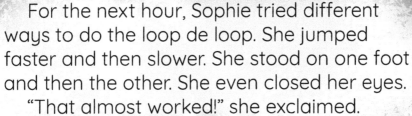

For the next hour, Sophie tried different ways to do the loop de loop. She jumped faster and then slower. She stood on one foot and then the other. She even closed her eyes. "That almost worked!" she exclaimed.

Just then, her mother peeked out the front door of their house.
"Time to get ready for bed, Sophie."

Sophie wiped the sweat from her forehead. "I'm so close," she told her mother. "Dad—you were right! If I just keep trying different things, I'll get it! While I'm falling asleep, I'm going to think about more things to try. And when I finally get it, Annie and I can do the loop de loop together!"

Sophie's parents leaned over and kissed Sophie's forehead as she hopped down the hall for her bath.

Mr. Owliver
ASKS

Do you know someone who can do something really well that you wish you could do too?

Have you tried something you wanted to do but couldn't do it?

What new activity would you try if you thought you could do it?

What are some different ways to do the thing you want to do?

To whom could you talk for help thinking of different ways to approach a new task?

Get more at pamburgess.com.

$\mathcal{About}$ THE AUTHOR

Pam Burgess lives with her husband on an inland lake in Michigan. She loves painting, photography, traveling, going to the movies and the theater, and playing with her grandchildren who live in Raleigh, North Carolina.

Pam is a lifelong learner who enjoys discovering new insights and perspectives.

In this book, Lochlan is named after Pam's third grandchild (pictured right).

CPSIA information can be obtained
at www.ICGtesting.com
Printed in the USA
BVHW012239100223
658310BV00005B/42

9 781953 259431